T0128720

BIO OF EMOTIONS

LAKEATHA HOOKER

authorHOUSE®

AuthorHouse™
1663 Liberty Drive
Bloomington, IN 47403
www.authorhouse.com
Phone: 1 (800) 839-8640

Published by AuthorHouse 04/13/2016

ISBN: 978-1-5246-0351-9 (sc)
ISBN: 978-1-5246-0350-2 (e)

Library of Congress Control Number: 2016906074

AMP
Scripture quotations marked AMP are from *The Amplified Bible*, Old Testament copyright © 1965, 1987 by the <u>Zondervan</u> Corporation. *The Amplified Bible*, New Testament copyright © 1954, 1958, 1987 by <u>The Lockman Foundation</u>. Used by permission. All rights reserved.

Print information available on the last page.

Any people depicted in stock imagery provided by Thinkstock are models, and such images are being used for illustrative purposes only. Certain stock imagery © Thinkstock.

This book is printed on acid-free paper.

We are here to open doors that were meant to be opened and lead a path for many others.

Reconcilicate Your Soul

Beauty of a statured heart; restored to sprout of a millions trees.

That field was once bare, with despair.

Tears and sacrifice of our Christ Savior gave life to the death that was forsaken to me.

There is no shame as it once hoarded.

The terror has fleed never to return.

Enemy! You have no reins… **BE GONE IN JESUS NAME!**

I am a child my Father God adores!

Everything I lost is blooming with the beauty of a million trees.

Sisters.

Brothers.

The Lord calls "come back to me".

Repent of your sins!

Rejoice!

Love from the healing of Christ healed me within.

Reconciliate your soul.

No longer broken as I feel the power of the Holy Spirit!

I sing praise as I am healed.

Healed! I am healed!

(Matthew 9:12-13 AMP Bible)
Jesus Christ did not come for the healthy, but to redeem the sick and broken.

Shollow Hill

The pain that cry's.
Shadows sallow your pain.
Till you sleep to die.
Fear not the darkness of night
still comes the day!
Light spreads to consume shadows hiding in the dark.
Lyrics to the pain that that cry's.
Pain that cry's.
Pain cry's; cry's to heal.
Heal from the pain, that cry's.
In the sallow hill.

Psalm 23:4(AMP Bible)
Yes, though I walk through the valley of the shadow of death,
I will fear or dread no evil, for You are with me; Your rod and
Your staff, they comfort me.

Cancer Leo Humor

Shorty don't play that! A smile that glows like fire, who loves like a child. Dare not spark my flame. Stay on my good side. I told you once and I will say it again. Shorty don't play that! Please remain as you are mannerable and composure in place. The stout of a body builder, charm of Casanova and Immense intellect. Temper of a wildcat with a sting like a bee. Think before you cross my path. I'm happy as can be. when necessary snappy with the claws of the Cancer and pouncing with the Leo in me. Shorty don't play that. Temp me and see!

God doesn't give up on you. Don't give up on yourself.

Food for the soul

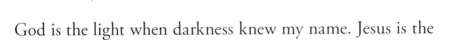

God is the light when darkness knew my name. Jesus is the star that shines as I sing.

The Holy Ghost is the presence that bound me to see.

I am a child of the most high God.

There is none that will ever forsake me.

In Jesus name I fall to my knees and pray "Thank you Father for the grace that has been given to me."

When darkness comes I shall fear no more.

Praise and Joy to my God I Adore.

Power does not propagate leadership character cultivates leaders.

Why do We Fall in Love

Our hearts engorge with joy even though we should run and hide.

The heavy hand of pain slaps our chest as our heart recovers from the blow.

The sound of the rhyme dies down to a small thump thump.

We are so weak to the additive emotion, that keeps you coming back.

As I intoxicated myself in the indulgence of love;

There was nothing or any one that could save me from it.

So why do we continue to crave this strong entrapping emotion?

We want what we cannot have.

The human heart is a fool for love.

Regardless of the pain that is caused.

Keep this in mind.

Love is not an emotion but an action or behavior or what you show to the one you adore.

When you learn to love; love is love and none of us can live without it.

You are what you believe.

Your Reflection

Daddy's little girl. I miss you so much. I miss telling you about my days; what life will be like when I grow up. Why did you leave me alone in this world without a man to teach me the ways of men preying on little girls? I dreamed of the day we'd come face to face. Your tender hearted sweet daddy's girl. The mind that inhabits your thoughts of a 11yr old. The misery I felt broke me when you left my world. Please come back; I need you Daddy's little girl. I love you Dad! You are my father the man that made half of me. Family even says that I'm the reflection you see. Just a grown woman trapped being Daddy's little girl. Come home to Daddy's little girl! Love has no end; you were my first friend. I'm just my Daddy's little girl! I love you Dad!

Looking in the mirror is easy. Its seeing your reflection that's a hard pill to swallow.

CHIME

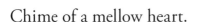

Chime of a mellow heart.
Cellulite painted frame hiding the hidden pain.
You don't know the anguish I feel! Judge not what comes from
dungeonous sin.
Words of condemnation weigh in.
Hatred thrust on the back of a homeless man!
Abhorrence beat down the skin of a colored child!
Resentment slapped the face of a poverty stricken family!
Labeled a terrorist garnished in insanity for praying in public!
Victimized simply for being a woman!
Persecuted by those I love.
Life is a gift; a blessing.
Vanquish the blinders that conceals clarity of sight.
Journey each day at a time.
A momentous occasion reverenced with love.
Judge not the sin of others; for so shall it come back judged
of the beginners ten times fold.
Uplift and encourage a broken soul.
Chimes once mellow, now bellow mending chimes.

_____

If you are not lead by truth you will die by a lie.

_____

Angel in Me

From the first day that I saw your face.
Your eyes had something to say.
Your smile sends comfort in an Angelic way.
I heard your voice as it caressed my heart.
Your touch is as soft as a cloud above in Heaven.
The tears from your pain gave you the strength to dig deep
inside for your resurrection.
When you read these words what do you see?
An angel without wings lives in me.

Revenge is best served with forgiveness!

Mark 11:25(AMP Bible)

And when you stand praying, if you hold anything against anyone, forgive them, so that your Father in heaven may forgive you your sins.

Abused

Bruises are more than skin deep.
I remember when you hit me.
You choose not to stop with the physical pain.
Sexual insults as I yell rape shocked me in shame.
A ruthless man with the gift of mind games.
I guess you didn't realize as careful not to leave marks…
Bruises live beyond skin deep.
The look in your eyes!
Mirrored Misery.
You are less than a man.
How could you abuse me?
You are worst then my worst enemy!
How could you?
Why would you?
Leave bruises that are more than skin deep.

If we wake up and served our purpose and see the light in the world how much better a world it would be!

Don't Be Dysfunctional

There is no proper fit. Things out of place. Your surroundings are unorganized. You might just be dysfunctional. You have anger in your heart with no interest of compromise. Sounds like you are dysfunctional. Can you count how many times you live selfishly, being dysfunctional? Your dysfunctional, dysfunctional, dysfunctional! Look in the mirror, you're not pleased with who you see. Change it up. Make things right. Remember to love self with sincerity and others you'll love easily. You are who you choose. You don't have to be dysfunctional, so don't be.

Winning is in your attitude.

I Love My Mama

On this very Special Day.
I have something that I like to say.
The road was hard and had many turns.
But a Mother's Love doesn't give up.
There are six of us that test your faith.
But the good Lord said" continue to pray".
I hope to someday make you proud.
So the glory of God will shine on you loud.
You are the most beautiful woman I have ever seen.
I am thankful to God that I was blessed!
To have a mother that shines of love from an Angels beam.

I love you, mama!

Don't complain in your goodness that you don't receive what you deserve. What we with flaws deserve, we are blessed not to receive.

Romans 8:1(AMP Bible)
There is therefore now no condemnation to them which are in Christ Jesus, who walk not after the flesh, but after the spirit.

Psalm 107:14(AMP Bible)
He brought them out of darkness and the shadow of death and broke apart the bonds that held them.

Do on to Others

We should respect each other as the individuals that we are.
Why is it so hard?
Treat others the way you expect to be treated.
Why is that so tuff?
Give love receive love and still it's not enough!
I didn't treat with or speak to you with disgust.
I am the friend that you always hoped I be.
You return all of this affection and admiration to the one that inflected pain deep beneath.
A hug, words of encouragement are best to receive.
For some reason that just escapes me.
The world refuses to see, that it is its own worst enemy!

A wise man cannot pass along wisdom if your words are filled with anger! Wisdom, Knowledge and Humility work hand and hand.

Proverbs 16:19(AMP Bible)
James 3:13(AMP Bible)
Luke 1:52(AMP Bible)
Psalm 138:6(AMP Bible)

Just Me

———⌘———

Five foot one I am. Can't take another closed door. A heart warmed to melt ice. Fear no man but I fear I'll never know God's plan. Take two steps forward; get knocked three steps back. Kids look to me to show what life is about. Nothing to fear but fear its self. Self-doubt is the evil haunting me. These words alive to keep me from dropping into depression. Locked in this cage of poverty; please let me out! With dreams of a successful life. Success grated from who God made me. Who am I?

I'm the woman that will keep moving forward.

I'm the woman that has a God given destiny!

I'm the women that is just me.

Help me, help me just be me! Help me, help me mineralize. I am she, she is me! I am she living out my God given destiny!

Let the pressure of life form the diamond in you.

Gratitude

Appreciation of your immaculate love will never be enough! I fall short of you and every day you pick me up. How you love me with the sacrifice of your life is beyond my thoughts. Lord I am grateful that you took my sins. If you only hear these words, please hear me say" I love you with tears in my eyes". I am flawed, sinful and prideful in my concentration and actions. I can't see in the dark. I'm so thankful you shined your light on me. In all my short comings you still died for me. Jesus Jesus Jesus! Please forgive me! I beg you to forgive me! Please except my apology. I live because you raised me from the dead.

Thank you Jesus!

Serve with a willing heart.
Serve with a grateful heart.
Serve with a humble heart.

Weathering Storm

When the storm comes, the sunshine stops. My happiness left with the season of joy. Life says the rainbow comes out to play, once the clouds dissipate away. I have no choice but to feel these words. The storm of life has run away with me. Joys rainbow holds on to me. Come home and be full of abundant elatement. Cry with the rain and sing praise to ease the pain. The day of your rainbow will come out to play.

Stop being comfortable with living uncomfortable.

Savior

I repent in the Lords name.
Our Messiah is the redeemer that leads me to seek tranquility
and justice for the weak.
Christ you came to me many times before.
Many times I hide in guilt of my sins.
Teacher you are the light I should not ignore.
I feel the warmth of my Lord's hand.
You are never and will not be without a home.
Home is with your father; this land you just visit.
Your love for others and trust in me has set you free for entity.
My savior, my savior I sing with glee!
Christ our Lord is the love that delivered me!

A little wisdom goes a long way.

Stand Tall

My days have been long.
The nights of rest are short.
I sometimes questioned if the fight was in me.
I cried out with a sigh!
As I embarked on this courageous journey I realized I'm not alone.
When my doubts were high and enthusiasm low; the grace of God shined on me to show.
I hear these words echo inside…
"You have wonderful family and friends that care".
Leave your pride and sadness at the door.
"Come on woman there is work to be done"!

You have the motivation to move mountains and mountains will move as they come.

Life goes on move with it. The past lives where it belongs and the future moves with the flow.

Sickness Calls

Nausea, lightheaded; weak with thoughts.
Never understanding the rage that hunts.
Those evil eyes plunge through my heart.
I swim in the sickened thoughts.
Oh please Lord shield me from harm.
I'm sick with shame because the enemy has diminished me.
I am not his first and not his last.
Flesh answers unwanted calls.
Praying his grip loosens this when sickness calls.
Strength from my spirit brings me to my feet.
I ignore the call that calls to me.
I have broken away from the sickness calls.
Thankful for the antidote.
The word of God saves with praise.

The only one that can hold you back is yourself.

Moods of A Cancer

Why does the soul cry till the moonshines?
The hollow wind dies.
When the sun comes out to play.
Maybe I'm just a spoiled child without the concept of limitations.
The mood swing of a cancer cannot be denied.
Sing what you feel.
Act what is real.
Never coward of the heart or you dare not heal.
Mood swings of a cancer are very real.
Real as the day will began and end.
Rainbow of wonder.
Shades of moods that Spector as captivated decorative views.
Why does the soul cry till the moon shines?
The hollow wind dies.
When the sun comes out to play.
The moods of a cancer sets the stage!

There are two types of relationships, reasons or seasons. Which one are you in? Learn from your reasons and enjoy your seasons.

Mourning Your Loss

Looking for you.
Where did you go?
Hurting at the loose of you.
Please don't go.
Memory's of your presence vanished from twelve years past.
I remember how gentle and free hearted it was to be you.
Tears are felt flowing a stream; remembering how your life was lost.
Daydreaming with thoughts; the impression of you to me.
I'll see you again at home in heaven.
Innocence in your beauty taken from me.
You may be gone but never forgotten.
You in children as they play.
A trace of innocence will always remain.
You are the farthest thing away from sin.
You are innocence.

Apply the knowledge you gain to multiply in wisdom. Your wisdom is your legacy.

Rhythm & Blues

Man of eloquent singing.
Oh how you sing the notes of seduction as you place women in a trance.
Queen of the Nile my Nubian Princess, you are a delicate flower of need of me.
These are the lyrics of temptation come flowing from your mouth.
Close your ears ladies the music draws near.
Mr. Casanova gives his performance with a lyre.
Reminiscing with passion as you began to fantasies.
Thinking about the lust that is seen in his eyes.
Wake up wake up!
The song you hear no more.
Illusions of passion and sin caused fallen victims to Jackal and Hide.
Man of performance seducing you of purity.
Eloquent man that sings the song "Rhythm and Blues".
Save your Rhythm and Blues".
Save your virtue.
Beware of the Jackal and Hide.
He comes with a devilish disguise.

Don't hold on to anger. Resolve the root source. Make peace and move forward.

Balla

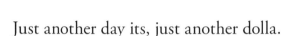

Just another day its, just another dolla.
You got to get out there and get your hustle on to be a balla.
Stakes are high.
The money is low.
Its maddening to the mind because your empty handed.
Cheddar ain't everything but everything is everything.
Stop for a minute!
What sense does this make?
It's a sad moment in time because your direction is weak.
What is more than just another day and just another dolla.
Gleam like a diamond smooth as a pearl.
Floss with the swag of a dime piece cover girl.
Just another day it's just another dolla.
Got to do it big in this material world.
Whatever my worth or the status I claim is not important, only my faith.
Ask me again and I say my friend.
It's never just another day another dolla.
The desire in me to seek the Lord's favor is all I need to feel like a balla.

I have enclosed a prayer that I've written. It has helped and continues to heal during my journey with the Lord. Prayer is an important part of healing. Healing is to restore as new or learning to relearn how to express emotions and actions.

A Prayer of Healing

Father I pray that you would please restore me daily. Each day I pray that you reveal your plan for me. Father I pray each wound that is yet to be seen, it be revealed so that it may be healed with your loving touch. Lead my need of healing. I pray that you light and encourage growth in me daily of your Will. May the Holy Spirit be with me to lead my heart where you shall have me procced. I know that nothing is wasted and I pray that you help me use that which was meant for my destruction to serve you whole heartedly and to heal. I thank you Father. In Jesus name Amen.

Jeremiah 17:14(AMP bible)
Heal me, O Lord, and I shall be healed; save me, and I shall be saved, for you are my praise.

Hebrew 11:6(AMP bible)
But without faith it is impossible to please and be satisfactory to Him. For whoever would come near to God exist and that He is the rewarder of those who earnestly and diligently seek Him out.

Acknowledgments

Thank you Father God for lighting the desire to step out my comfort zone. There is no love like the love of Jesus. It is through Jesus that I am healed. I love my children and my little cousin Kenosha, Daiza, Jaden and Anailea; you four are truly blessings and inspiration. Thank you, family and friends for your encouragement and support. You have made a difference. I love you all.

Printed in the United States
By Bookmasters